THE TEENAGER'S GUIDEBOOK

Answers to the most common questions on your teenager's mind

THE TEENAGER'S GUIDEBOOK

Copyright © 2020 by **Elijah Fagorala**

ISBN: 978-1-952098-02-4

Cornerstone Publishing

A Division of Cornerstone Creativity Group LLC
Phone: +1(516) 547-4999
info@thecornerstonepublishers.com
www.thecornerstonepublishers.com

To order bulk of this book or to contact the author for speaking engagement, please email:

elijahfagorala@gmail.com

CONTENTS

ACKNOWLEDGMENTS

Firstly, I give all the glory and honor to my Maker, in whom all wisdom lies, for the inspiration to write this book.

Many thanks to my supportive wife who added her motherly flair to the book. I appreciate my growing kids who prompted the need to write this book.

I am grateful to my family and friends for your immense contributions. I thank all members of the Cornerstone Publishing team - what a journey with me. Thank you for being a part of this chapter of my life!

INTRODUCTION

Anyone who has ever raised a child to adulthood can readily testify that the most difficult time in parenting is when children are in their teenage years. A chain of physical, psychological and behavioral changes occurs within this period that baffles not only the teenagers themselves but also their parents. These changes mainly come from the biological preparation of their brain and body for adulthood. Curiously, however, the manifestations of these changes are quicker and more visible in certain areas of their lives than the others. For instance, while growth hormones catalyze rapid growth in their physical forms, the regions of their brains responsible for sound judgment, thoughtfulness, patience and foresightedness take some time to form.

Similarly, just as these youngsters develop tendencies that make them to withdraw and seek independence from their parents, while forming a closer attraction and responsiveness to their peers, they are at this time much more vulnerable to criticisms, negative influences, low self-esteem and depression. This ironically makes them to need the support, guidance and encouragement of their parents more than ever, even if they do not show it. Sadly, ignorance of the complexities of this phase of life has turned many parents and guardians into frustrated and despairing combatants, rather than the enlightened and understanding guides that the teenagers expect them to be.

Truth be told, it would be unfair to totally blame the present generation of parents for the misunderstanding that erupts between them and their teenagers. Indeed, many parents, having once been teenagers themselves, often do their best to brace up for the challenges that come with parenting teens, with the determination to make it a wonderful time for themselves and their beloved children. However, a good number of these parents end up being bewildered by the rapidity of the changes in their children's attitude, as well as the effrontery with which these once obedient children suddenly begin to challenge parental authority. What propels this unexpected behavior, most times, is the monumental pressures and influences that the current generation of children face from external forces, such as the social media, which people from the older generation did not experience.

Naturally, as the disconnect and rifts between them and their parents grow deeper, teenagers easily find solace and encouragement in their peers, celebrity role models and social media "influencers" – who, in most cases, give them wrong counsels and examples to follow. It is in consideration of this widening gulf between teenagers and their parents and other caretakers that this book has been written. It covers most of the fundamental questions rattling the minds of teenagers but which they are often afraid to ask their parents, for fear of being misunderstood, sermonized or considered eccentric. It also simplifies the task of parents by not only helping them to understand what is going in their teenagers' minds but providing ready-made answers that can be adopted or adapted, as the occasion requires.

It is my belief that by knowing what their children are curious or concerned about, parents will be more relaxed, patient, understanding and better equipped in guiding, helping and bringing out the best in their teenagers, rather than being alienated from them.

PART 1

ABOUT YOUR IDENTITY

1

WHY SHOULD I BELIEVE IN MYSELF?

Some time ago, there was a young woman who used to be so sad about the color of her hair and her height. She used to envy many of her peers who had a different hair color and were taller. She desperately wished she could be like them. There were times she even prayed to God to change her, but nothing happened.

Years later she became dedicated to the work of evangelism. At a time, she received the call to take the gospel message to another country and live with the people. Surprisingly, when she got to the strange land, she realized that most of the people had her color of hair and were about her size in height. These physical similarities with the natives really endeared them to her and made it easy for them to receive her and the message she had brought to them.

It was at this time she realized why God had refused to answer her previous prayers over her physical looks. God had made her in a special way because she had a very special assignment to fulfill on earth. This is the same way you too must look at yourself from now on. God sees you as a special person and you must accept, appreciate and live with the consciousness of this truth at all times.

Just as the Psalmist says in Psalm 139:14, you have been "fearfully and wonderfully made." Regardless of the circumstances of your birth or your family background; regardless of your looks or level of intelligence, God made and sees you as a special person. You know why? It is primarily because you are unique. You are beautiful, awesome and loaded with potentials and possibilities. There is no other person like you in the whole world. Even science confirms your uniqueness. If you check your fingerprints, irises, retinas and some other parts of your body, you will find that nobody else in the entire world has what you have.

All of these, plus the fact that you have a unique DNA should make you know that you are not a worthless or accidental creature. And you certainly are not a result of mass production process. God took his time to determine everything about you – including your physical attributes, the time, place and circumstances of your birth, as well as some of the experiences that have shaped your life up to this point.

And do you know why God would devote so much time to your life? It is because you have an assignment to fulfil for Him on earth. This means that your birth or existence is not a random occurrence. You should believe in yourself and your worth because you are a carrier of God's mandate. There is something He has deposited in you that no one else can do. You have your unique path, talent and destiny. So you need not envy any of your peers because your life is different from theirs. Your mission on earth is different. Let me repeat – you are not a wanderer on earth; you are a wonder, waiting to happen!

You must also believe in yourself because this is the only way you can achieve anything meaningful in life and fulfil your purpose. There is a saying that you may succeed if no one else believes in you, but can never succeed if you don't believe in yourself. What you believe about yourself will go a long way in determining what becomes of your life. This is why Henry Ford said, "Whether you think you can or think you can't, you are right."

Another reason you have to believe in yourself is because you will be faced with many challenges and oppositions on your path to destiny. You will hear many discouraging things from people that should have been your best fans and encouragers. The only thing that will keep you going then is the belief you have in your vision and the faith you have in God.

You should also feel good and happy because God's got your back at any time. Everybody else may see nothing good in you and consider you a total failure, but God sees the best in you at all times – including the times you make mistakes.

So, look away from all limitations, oppositions and difficulties all around you, and look at the bright future ahead of you. Focus on your strengths, not on your weakness. Concentrate on what you have, not on what you don't. Meditate on who is for you – God Almighty – not those who are against you. As long as God is on your side, you can do anything, conquer anything and become anything!

2

WHY SHOULD I BELIEVE IN GOD AND CREATIONISM?

Truth be told, the subject of the existence of God and His role in the creation of the universe shouldn't be one to be debated, considering that, like every manufacturer or creative genius, the imprint of God is upon the entire creation. For humans, in particular, who are said to be the crown of God's creation, the God-consciousness seems to have been deliberately implanted in us, perhaps due to the foreknowledge of God about what human beings were capable of becoming.

One of the clearest demonstrations of this God-consciousness is our instinctive inclination towards morality – the principles of right and wrong. The majority of human beings are appalled by wrongs like injustice, cruelty and criminality; while we are delighted by rights, such as justice, kindness and goodness. These are principles that have no basis or explanations in science. They only find meaning and explanations in subjects relating to God.

I will return to this issue of morality later; but for now, let's deal with the undeniable reality that beginning mainly from the time known as the Age of Reason, people have increasingly disputed the existence of God. And quite naturally, His place in the origin of the universe has been repeatedly denied as well. It may interest you to know that the Age of Reason began around the 18th century and was marked by a major shift in people's perception about humanity and the universe as a whole. Eager to liberate themselves from the excesses of religion and superstition that characterized the Middle Ages, people began to embrace the exaggerated belief in man's perfection and autonomy, as well as his potential to place himself at the center of the universe through his superior thinking ability.

As you might expect, with this frenzy to do away with anything God or religion also came changes in scientific thought and exploration. Different ideas began to emerge as substitutes for biblical truths in explanation of natural phenomena. It was from here that it became popular to use scientific ideas to counter beliefs in God and creationism. To prove their points, many scientists have, from that period, come up with theories to try to explain how the universe and all the creatures in it came into existence. Chief among these explanations is the evolution theory – which, basically says that life came to be by accident and has continued to evolve on its own, without the involvement of any higher power.

I am sure you must have come across this theory at school or elsewhere. And, with the aggressive way in which the theory is being forced on students in schools, it is possible for even the strongest believer in the existence of God and His power in the creation process to begin to question his or her beliefs and convictions. But before you do so, there are a few things for you to consider.

The first thing you should consider is the confusion among the evolutionists as to how exactly this evolution has happened over time. There used to be a group, led by French scientist, Georges Cuvier, that believed that evolution began through violent catastrophic events or "revolutions" that had contributed to extinction of old species and the development of species to replace them in the newly created environment. Then came English geologist, Charles Lyell, who said that evolution had been influenced by slow changes since the beginning of time in the shape of the terrestrial surface that could not be perceived by the human eye. After that came Charles Darwin, who based his theory of evolution on the concepts of natural selection and survival of the fittest.

There are so many more schools of thought on this so-called evolution process. Beyond their inconsistencies, however, it would interest you to know that none of these evolution theorists – from the most ridiculous to the most popular – can give a precise answer on how life actually began. If, for instance, we were to accept the claim that life began through some "catastrophic events or revolutions", the question is, what or who triggered these events? Or if we were to believe that evolution is aided by some "slow changes", then we would need to ask, changes from what? And for the perspective of Darwin, we cannot talk about the survival of the fittest, without clearly knowing how the fit and the unfit came to be, in the first place.

The point is, only in God and His word can we find a definitive answer to the creation question. At best, scientists can only speculate on it. As one of the greatest scientists of all time, Sir Isaac Newton, once admitted: "Gravity explains the motions of the planets, but it cannot explain who sets the planets in motion." Only God's word provides such answer.

The second thing I want you to consider is the evolutionists' claim that the wonders, the orderliness, the beauty and the organic complexity that we see both in ourselves as humans and in the universe as a whole came from some Big Bang explosion or that they just happened by chance. The following two perspectives, provided by youngsters like you, show clearly why you can't afford to fall for these evolutionists' claims: "Imagine that someone told you that there was an explosion at a printing plant and that the ink spattered onto the walls and ceilings and formed an unabridged dictionary. Would you believe it? How much more unbelievable is it that everything in the orderly universe came about as a result of a random big bang?"

""If you were walking through the forest and discovered a beautiful log cabin, would you think: 'How fascinating! The trees must have fallen in just the right way to make this house.' Of course not! It's just not reasonable. So why should we believe that everything in the universe just happened to come about?""

Thirdly, you should consider that despite the claim by evolutionists that higher organisms evolved from the lower ones, there are still so many lower organisms and even the most "basic" forms of life that are so complex in their structures, just like human beings. And then you might also wonder why the intellectual abilities of human beings are much more advanced than those of apes, from whom evolutionists claim that we emerged.

Fourthly, you must consider that accepting the claim that life came by accident means that life is altogether meaningless. It means that our lives have no value, purpose or direction as individuals. It means that the years we spend trying to acquire education, get a job, start a family and raise children are wasted and worthless. Isn't this frustrating and hopeless? Well, that's what evolutionists would have us believe but cheeringly, things are different from the perspective of God. According to God's word, you came from somewhere and you are heading somewhere. All your steps, choices and decisions are meaningful and they contribute to the eventual outcome of your life. Isn't this more assuring?

Fifthly, it goes without saying that if life came by accident and is therefore meaningless, then we shouldn't have to abide by moral codes or have laws regulating our lives as human beings. If life is meaningless and we all are merely trying to survive, why pay attention to moral principles? Why don't we all live like amoral creatures and do whatever we can to survive, regardless of what happens to other people's feelings? Why do we have to bother about how others feel before we act? Why do we reward good deeds and punish wrongdoers? Isn't it the God-nature in us that propels this or is there an aspect of evolution theory or science as a whole that explains why we need laws to have a peaceful, orderly, decent and progressive society?

As you consider these realities and many more, you would come to the understanding that while science has helped the human race in many ways, it still cannot provide all the answers to the questions of mankind or solutions to our myriads of problems. Only in God can we find ultimate answers and solutions.

3

WHY AM I ON EARTH?

This is one of the most important questions anyone can ask in life. In fact, I think it's the most important. So if you are asking it now in your early years, I congratulate you – with the hope that you are asking it with the sincere desire to make a meaning out of your life and not like so many people who ask it in despair and use it as an excuse to end their lives. Even if you are among this second group and you're beginning to think life is meaningless, I congratulate you because you have a chance to be reading this and you are willingly doing so.

Now, why do I think this is the most important question in life? It is because the answer to it is what gives your life purpose and direction and it is what determines whether you find fulfilment in life or not. This is why someone said that the two most important days of your life are the day you were born and the day you discover the reason why. Yes, there is a unique purpose for your life. And it is important you find and fulfil it. As Thomas Carlyle, British historian and teacher, once said, "A man without a purpose is like a ship without a rudder- a waif, a nothing, a no man. Have a purpose in life, and, having it, throw such strength of mind and muscle into your work as God has given you."

I want you to observe two things from the above quote. The first is that life often seems empty, meaningless and worthless until you find your purpose. This is why many people live recklessly and involve themselves in activities that can ruin them and others. They don't really value their lives because it doesn't seem to be beyond the daily routines that people generally engage in. This gets boring over time and some devise all sorts of means to fill the void in their lives. This is the reason many go into drugs, immoral sex and alcoholism. Unfortunately, as many discover – often when it's too late – these supposed remedies only end up compounding their frustration. Eventually, many end up taking their own lives.

Take the example of Richard Barton who was a famous cartoonist and seemed to be enjoying life until the day he took his own life. He left this note before he did: "I have had few difficulties, many friends, great successes; I have gone from wife to wife, from house to house, visited great countries of the world, but I am fed up with inventing devices to fill up twenty-four hours of the day." This is similar to what many other people who commit suicide or those merely hanging on to life express or just hide within themselves.

The second and most important truth from that quote is that purpose comes from God. Yes, that is the truth and this is where many get it wrong. You cannot live a meaningful and fulfilled life without God. God specially made and equipped you with special abilities (gifts and talents) so you can make a specific and significant contribution to the world. It is important therefore that you have a personal relationship with God, so He can reveal your assignment on earth to you and also show you how to succeed at it.

Let me tell you a story to illustrate this. Several years ago, a young man driving a Ford vehicle experienced much difficulty when the vehicle broke down by the side of a road. This man knew a lot about cars and specifically this car, so he went to work. He tried different things and each time he went back to try and crank the engine, it still wouldn't start. He tried tricks things and, still, nothing happened. The car just wouldn't start.

A few minutes later, a large limousine pulled up beside him. Out stepped an old man who just stood and watched the struggling young man for a few minutes. Finally, the old man looked at him and told him to adjust a specific part of the engine. The young man was initially skeptical as it seemed unreasonable to him that the part mentioned by the old man could have caused the vehicle to break down.

But then, after considering that he had tried other options without succeeding, he thought he might as well give the old man's advice a shot. So he adjusted the part, got in the car and sure enough, the engine cranked to life. He was surprised and asked the old man, "How did you know what to do?" The old man said, "My name is Henry Ford and I invented this car."

This is how your life is meant to function. God made you and knows all you need to live a happy, successful and fulfilled life. Your life is not useless and you are not here accidentally. You are here to fulfil God's assignment, which is why you must search within yourself and reach out to Him in sincerity so you can be guided to find the meaning of your life. As Rick Warren says, "You were made for a mission. You aren't here just to wander around lost. And you aren't here simply to live for yourself."

Seek your purpose in God, and you will find it.

4

WHY CAN'T I DROP OUT OF SCHOOL?

I understand that going to school and keeping to all its rules and meeting its demands can be much of a pain sometimes. But then again, isn't that how life in itself is structured? Nothing good comes easy and there's no gain without some pain. This is the same path that all of the great men and women who have made remarkable success in their chosen careers or vocations have followed. This is why someone said, "Someday you will look back on your life and realize that everything worthwhile you've ever accomplished initially challenged you. And that is as it should be, because big challenges often prepare ordinary people for extraordinary success."

What you are getting in school will not only last you for a lifetime but will also open the door for you to live an enviable life, accomplish great things and fulfil your dreams. You certainly cannot expect such a master key to simply get into your hands without paying the price.

The price for a sound, balanced and enriching education is a combination of determination and perseverance. With each of the efforts made to teach and train you, you are gradually climbing your way out of ignorance and stepping into heights of knowledge, understanding and unlimited opportunities. Now, tell me, which is easier – to climb up or to drop down? Of course, it is to climb!

So, whatever issues you may be having in school now, dropping out isn't the solution. In fact, it is like jumping out of the frying pan into the fire. Of course, dropping out may seem like the easiest way out at first, but it eventually comes with a lot of pain, regrets and difficulties. I will share some of these with you.

The first thing you should know is that in dropping out of school, it becomes much more difficult for you to enjoy the better life and amazing future you've always yearned for. Getting a good job becomes extremely difficult because most employers prefer to hire someone who has successfully completed some level of education – at least a diploma – than to get someone who dropped out of school. According to data from the Bureau of Labor Statistics, high school dropouts are having a harder time finding and keeping jobs than individuals with higher levels of education. In fact, the national unemployment rate for high school dropouts in July 2009 was 15.4 percent, compared to 9.4 percent for high school graduates, 7.9 percent for individuals with some college credits or an associate's degree, and 4.7 percent for individuals with a bachelor's degree or higher.

Also, in a recent report published by the World Bank about Tunisia, a country in Africa, it is stated: "About 140,000 students drop out of school annually, 80,000 of whom have not completed their basic education (Ben Romdhane 2010). Two-thirds of these dropouts obtain no further training and to varying degrees, generally find themselves in exploitative forms of casual labor. Often, they express a degree of bitterness or regret at having left school…"

Secondly, if you drop out of school now, your chances of getting any form of formal education later on become really slim. Since you are supposed to move from one level of education to another, dropping out of high school or college, for instance, means that you cannot obtain a higher qualification. It means you can never get a diploma or degree and would have cut yourself off from the beautiful experiences and opportunities that these would have offered you. For instance, being a dropout means that you are less likely to receive job-based health insurance. And without access to health insurance, you may not receive crucial preventive health care that can lower the possibility of you having a chronic disease and increasing your lifespan.

Thirdly, as it is said that the idle mind is the devil's workshop, dropping out of school will make you more likely to get into associations, behaviors and influences that will prove harmful to your life and destiny. According to a report, "The increased likelihood of poverty, along with the decreased access to higher education and career opportunities makes high school dropouts susceptible to crime and possibly substance abuse. An astonishing 80 percent of incarcerated individuals did not complete high school. And as of 2013, 31 percent of high school dropouts used drugs compared to 18 percent of high school graduates. Because many of those dropouts don't have health insurance and may be sentenced to prison at some point, the costs of treatment fall to the taxpayer."

Most importantly, dropping out of school can mean that your ability to endure difficulty and devise survival strategies is very low. This puts you at a serious disadvantage because it will also become very difficult for you to achieve success in any other meaningful thing you try to do. As already said above, any worthwhile achievement in life comes with some level of challenges and if you consider dropping out as a solution to the challenges you are facing in school now, what is the guarantee that you will not drop out of a job, a marriage or a business?

So, if you have concerns or problems with your going to school now, you can discuss with your parents or teachers or get a good counselor and they will advise you on the best decision to take to solve the problems. You can overcome any obstacle and conquer any challenge once you are determined to do it. As it is rightly said, where there is a will, there is always a way. So, hang on there, till you find a way to overcome. Yes, you can!

PART 2

ABOUT YOUR OUTLOOK

5

WHY DO I HAVE TO WEAR THIS TYPE OF CLOTHING?

I recently read an article on a website and it paints a graphic picture of one of the major reasons your parents sometimes disapprove of your choice of clothing or style of dressing. Here is the first paragraph: "One Sunday, walking up a flight of steps in our church auditorium, I encountered two teenage girls sitting on the stairway. Not only were they blocking traffic, they sat in a most immodest way in short skirts, revealing far more than they knew. I grieved, knowing how difficult it would be for men and boys going up those stairs…"

I also read about a man standing off to the side, in front of a church, dressed in baggy, torn clothes, unshaven and very unkempt. As the members went into the church, they had to pass this man. Not one member stopped to greet him. All ignored him and looked the other way because of his suspicious looks. Surprisingly, however, the following week, the pastor announced that he was the man who had been in front of the church the previous week, dressed in old clothes!

What do these scenarios tell you? There is a lot more consideration you must make in your dressing, aside from the feeling of being trendy and attracting flattering comments from a few of your peers. You must understand that the way you are dressed says a lot about you, or rather tells people what you want them to think of you. This is why it is advised that you must dress the way you wish to be addressed.

Of course, there is also a saying that you don't judge a book by its cover. But the reality is that human beings are wired to associate appearance with personality. And you cannot totally blame them. People in different professions, for example, have their uniforms or way of dressing, which makes it easy for anyone to identify them. Doctors, nurses, chefs, police officers, soldiers, astronauts, firemen, sportsmen, clergymen, pop stars, and even sex workers all have their special way of dressing and presenting themselves to the world.

This means, for example, that if you are not a cop but are dressed like one, people are likely to mistake you for one. The same will happen if you were to dress like a nurse, even if you were not one. Sadly, the same is true in negative cases. If you were dressed the way a sex worker would dress – revealing very sensitive parts of your body – it is very easy to be seen, addressed and treated as one, which you will definitely find embarrassing. Also, as a young man, if you were to dress like a hooligan or a gangster, that's the way most people are likely to relate with you, regardless of what other positive qualities you may have to offer.

The point here is that, with your dressing and appearance, you teach people how to treat you. Either you teach them to treat you with respect or you teach them to treat you with disrespect. Here is the instructive experience of a young lady, called Christi, as reported by the Christian Broadcasting Network (CBN):

When I first began working as a Christian summer camp counselor, I decided that I would refuse to hook up with a guy at camp so I could focus wholeheartedly on the girls in my cabin. I wanted so much for them to like me and to think I was cool that I dressed in the latest young fashions… snug-fitting, low-rise jeans, short shorts, spaghetti-strap tank tops, or tops that were short and clingy enough to resemble the popular crop tops when I was moving around, but long enough that I couldn't be accused of dressing inappropriately. I also taught the girls how to do several of the latest dance moves each night in the cabin, something we all looked forward to and had a lot of fun with.

I succeeded in being well liked by the girls at camp, but I also had the attention and admiration of some of the male camp counselors. I decided that I could just play it cool and clown around with these guys. They chased me around with water guns, gave me piggyback rides to the cafeteria, slipped ice down the back of my shirt, and fun stuff like that. I kept asking them to please leave me alone so I could concentrate on my girls, but they rarely respected my requests, no matter how firm I was.

I complained to one of the other counselors about how the guys were distracting me from what I came to do. She put her hand on mine and sweetly said, "Christi, your actions speak louder than your words. Even though you don't intend to dress to catch guys, they can't avoid noticing you dressing the way you do. If you dress like a cute little plaything and present yourself as a toy, then boys will be boys and try to play with that toy!"

So, when your parents express concern about your dressing, they are mostly concerned about three things, which are all in your interest: modesty, neatness and suitability. They do not want you to have sensitive parts of your body showing and attracting the wrong attention; of course, at the same time, they do not want you appearing scruffy, unkempt or looking like a granny. They also want you to look neat and responsible, and to show that you are coming from a decent home. And they equally want you to dress in ways that are fitting for occasions and weather conditions, so you don't end up getting ill or embarrassed.

6

WHY CAN'T I BUY THIS TYPE OF PHONE?

It was reported in the media, a few years back, that a young schoolgirl of about 15 years of age had been shot dead on the streets by robbers who wanted to dispossess her of her expensive phone. Her parents were, to say the least, devastated when they were called to identify her. I can imagine that one of the thoughts that must have crossed their minds at that heartbreaking moment was: Wouldn't things have been different if she had been in possession of a cheaper and much inferior phone?

Of course, you may consider this an extreme example of the threats that having a phone, especially a smartphone, by a teenager poses. After all, how many teenagers get attacked because of their expensive phones? The truth however is that there are a number of reasons why your loving parents may not want you to have a particular kind of phone.

Before detailing some of these likely reasons, let me say

that that, as a teenager, there are very good reasons why you may want to have a phone in the first place. A phone will be useful in communicating with your parents, when either you or they are away from each other, and it is also vital for staying in touch with your friends, relatives and loved ones. So, basically, it can prevent boredom, keep you informed and provide some form of security, especially in case of an emergency. Your cell phone can also connect you to a practically infinite pool of knowledge and ideas that can enlighten and empower you, as well as broadening your worldview and assisting you to tackle your school work.

But, then, your parents may also be worried that getting you a certain kind of phone may get you addicted to some of its features to the detriment of your health, studies and even relationship with them and others. As one parent said, "We wanted our children to spend their time playing outside. And reading books. And talking with us. So we never bought them phones. They kept getting older, and we kept not buying them phones. Now that they are in middle and high school, I realize that their childhood has been somewhat different from their friends'—and also remarkably different from mine."

Addiction to smartphone has been identified as the reason many youngsters are failing or getting low grades at school. Besides, being in possession of a phone could open up avenues for unwholesome interactions with people of suspicious character, which could expose you to cyber bullying and other online threats. This could be one of the concerns of your parents.

Additionally, your parents may be worried that you would be pressured by your peers into doing certain things that you wouldn't have done ordinarily, or with another kind of phone. For instance, a study found that 22% of teenage girls and 20% of teenage boys had sent nude or semi-nude pictures of themselves over the Internet or from their cell phones. The painful reality is that once such pictures are sent out there, they can be posted to a social website or sent to every cell phone in the school. Sexting, as this is sometimes called, can lead to your reputation being ruined forever.

Your parents may also be concerned about the cost of the phone, as well as becoming the unhappy recipient of a huge monthly bill. They may wonder, why spend so much on a phone when there are more important things that should take the money? Moreover, it is absolutely true that life is in phases and there is a time for everything. Your priority now as a teenager shouldn't be to use the best phone or compete with others on who gets the latest phone first. Your primary focus should be making the best grades and achieving your academic dream. After that, you can get a job and decide what you spend your money on, including what you can spare to buy a phone.

And just like the case in the opening story, your parents may be equally concerned about having unwanted attention drawn to you simply because of the kind of phone you have. So, they may disagree with your request – not necessarily because they want to deprive you, but because they want to protect you.

7

WHY SHOULD I BE CAREFUL WITH SOCIAL MEDIA?

The short answer to this is that the social media never forgets or forgives your blunders. Here is a touching proof. In April 2013, 17-year-old Paris Brown became UK's first ever youth police and crime commissioner. Her job was to advise the Police and Crime Commissioner on issues affecting youngsters in the country. She was to be on a salary of £15000 (that's over $19,000) a year.

Sadly, however, just six days after, Brown was forced to resign her appointment, due to the widespread criticisms she received over some of the comments she had tweeted from when she was 14 years old to when she was 16. Someone had gone to dig up the tweets, which many considered racist, and thus arose a wave of backlash that eventually saw her quitting after being continually hounded and harassed.

Her resignation statement was particularly sad but instructive. Part of it read: "I accept that I have made comments on social networking sites which have offended many people and I am really, truly sorry for any offence that has been caused... I have fallen into the trap of behaving with bravado on social networking sites. I hope that this stands as a learning experience for many other young people."

There are countless other cases throughout the world of young people who paid or are paying heavily for being careless on the Internet. This is why you should appreciate it when your parents try to restrict your presence on the various social media platforms.

Don't get me wrong though; there are lots of benefits you can get from the social media. It helps you to connect and stay in touch with friends, thereby reducing loneliness and boredom. It helps you connect with family members and loved ones that are in faraway places. You are also informed about current affairs, as well getting useful ideas, expressing yourself freely and also having some fun.

The challenge, however, comes from the fact that, except you consciously exercise caution, social media may soon become a controlling force in your life – and that's where the oodles of troubles associated with it begin to manifest. First is the potential negative effect on your studies and social life. Most social media platforms are designed to keep you engaged with frequent notifications about updates and messages. And in your attempt to keep up with these updates, you may find yourself focusing less on your studies and home works. This is why students who are heavy social media users tend to have lower grades.

On the social side, know that addiction to social media can actually make you become anti-social. You will find yourself isolating yourself the more and preferring to chat online, while ignoring communication with people who are within your immediate environment.

The second challenge is the possible effect on your emotional life. You could get so attached to the social media that it begins to determine your daily mood. You may find yourself constantly basing your worth and right to happiness on how much acceptance and approval (likes and retweets) you get on social media. Consequently, days when you get the most likes and attention on social media become your happy days, while you become moody, gloomy and irritable on other days.

It is also not surprising that having discovered the impact of social media comments on the moods of people, many have taken it as an opportunity to engage in cyberbullying. Cyberbullies use the social media to taunt and bully others. It is easier to bully through social media than to do it physically. Due to the huge level of networking offered by social media, cyberbullying moves from bad to worse in a matter of days causing long-lasting pains. In fact, social media has been a major cause of depression, anxiety, low self-esteem, eating disorders and even suicide among many youths.

One other challenge with social media is the pressure to be like other teenagers. It's very easy to feel like the odd one out when you see many of your peers posting pictures of what they do and where they visit on social media. Some of the things you see may be immoral or illegal, but you will feel like they are trendy. Added to this is the feeling that you need to go out of your way to impress others, so as to get likes and give the impression that you're having the best of fun and enjoyment. This is why many youngsters use photoshop, "filters" and some other tools to present themselves differently from what they are in reality. In extreme cases, many youngsters have died or been involved in life-changing accidents in the process of trying to take the "perfect selfie" in very dangerous places.

Social networks are also filled with criminals and predators, whose mission is to take advantage of young minds and lure them into evils or simply ruin their lives by raping them or harming them in some other ways. It is for these reasons that clinical psychologist and author of *The Teen Girl's Survival Guide*, Dr. Lucie Hemmen counsels, "Most people experience huge benefits from taking a social media break. There is a way in which cultivating and maintaining your online identity can replace an authentic connection to your true self. The more grounded you are in your authentic value as a human being, the less likely you are to be a heavy user of social media and also to be negatively affected by it."

Please, take caution from this and save your life and wellbeing.

8

WHY SHOULD I OBEY MY SCHOOL'S DRESS CODE?

One of the most disturbing trends in recent times is the rate at which students blatantly seek to rebel against school rules and regulations. Even worse is that in some cases, their parents not only condone but also encourage such behaviors as can be seen in the way they react when disciplinary measures are taken against such students by the school authorities. So, if you have parents who advise and encourage you to abide by school rules and regulations, you are among the lucky teenagers around.

Before I tell you the general benefits of obeying your school rules, let me dwell a bit on the reasons schools have uniforms for students. It is possible that, like many other teenagers, you detest having to wear a uniform to school and don't see why the uniform policy should exist in the first place, much less abiding by them. But here are some reasons your school requires students to wear a uniform.

- Uniforms serve to make all students socially equal. This means that uniforms ensure that no student feels superior or inferior to the other. Since all wear the same thing, there is no immediate social barrier and all can see one another as equal peers. This, of course, prevents the possibility of a student being picked upon for bullying because of his or choice of dressing.

- Uniforms keep many students from misbehaving outside of the school premises because they know that their uniforms will easily reveal their school and that could put them in serious trouble. An education expert noted that uniforms often directly contribute to a feeling of school pride, which students do not want to compromise by misbehaving outside the school gate.

- Since uniforms help to immediately identify youngsters as students and mostly minors, it helps people to be more alert and conscious of their vulnerable status and thus be concerned for their safety and conduct. Some students once reported that security guards were more likely to follow them around shops if they were wearing their uniforms.

- Uniforms help to save the time and energy that students would have had to expend every morning on deciding which clothes to wear to school.

- Uniforms also help students to focus more on their studies and be more attentive in class because the distraction that comes with worrying over the attractiveness or otherwise of what they are wearing is taken away. They can listen to their teachers and contribute more in class without feeling that all eyes are on them because of their choice of clothes.

- Uniforms also help to put less pressure on parents. Sometimes, out of peer pressure, teenagers tend to demand that their parents buy them the trendiest clothes, which are often the most expensive.

- Similarly, it puts less pressure on the school authorities because they spend less time deciding the appropriateness or otherwise of what students wear to school.

- Schools have different policies as to the type, color, and style of uniforms their students can wear and they are often strict about such policies; so it is good you comply with them to avoid disciplinary measures and avoidable embarrassment. But beyond that is the need for you to understand the importance of respecting rules. You see, repeated actions become habits and your habits make up your character, while your character often determines how far you are able to go in life and where you eventually end your life's journey.

- What this means therefore is that you have to learn from now that life operates by rules and principles. You just cannot escape rules in life. God, who made the world, has rules and principles He has put in place to regulate our behaviors towards one another and towards Him. These principles also help to ensure the preservation of the universe and all its inhabitants. We call some of these principles "natural laws", which when altered, often result in serious consequences.

- It is the same with all countries, states, counties, communities, institutions and organizations all over the world. There are rules and regulations, which are contained in constitutions, codes of conduct, ethics and so on. These regulations help to maintain order, harmony, peace, justice, fairness, stability, identity, progress and prosperity in the different human settings and environment. More importantly, it is these rules that sometimes differentiate human communities from jungles. In other words, without these laws in place, things will go bad and none can be guaranteed safety.

- Now, why is this important to you? Well, if you find it difficult to abide by simple rules and regulations laid down by your school now, then you may have problems being a law-abiding citizen or abiding by any other regulations in other settings. You will find it hard to obey traffic rules or conform to professional ethics or immigration requirements. Eventually, you may end up causing lots of problems for yourself and constituting a threat to the peace and safety of others.

So, learn to start respecting rules and boundaries now, so that it can become a part of you as you make progress in life.

PART 3

ABOUT YOUR HEALTH

9

WHY CAN'T I SMOKE?

Let me begin by asking you why you want to smoke. Is it because you see adults all around you smoking and you are drawn to it? Is it because you see your mates in school or in the neighborhood or in movies doing it? Is it because you consider it a way of showing that you are old enough to do whatever you want? Or is it simply because you consider it a fun-filled adventure or a cheap way to get high?

Whatever your motivation or reason may be, you must be aware that behind the appearance of fun, adventure or relief in smoking lies a multitude of health risks that can affect you in unimaginable ways. In actual fact, smoking is dangerous for all age groups. This is why cigarette manufacturers are mandated to attach a health warning to their advertisements. The reason is because all health experts universally agree that smoking is a death trap. But the risks are much higher for teenagers.

The first thing you should know is that smoking is a very addictive habit. Once you start, it is very difficult for you to stop. This is because nicotine, the chemical that gets people high when they smoke, is very addictive. Just like cocaine, heroin and other similar drugs, the body and mind quickly get used to the nicotine in cigarettes. So, if you think you can try it briefly and then stop once you know what it feels like, then know that things may not work according to your plans. As soon as your body gets the feel of nicotine, it keeps demanding for it, till you start feeling abnormal and restless without a stick of cigarette.

If you have the opportunity to question most of the grown-ups who are hooked to smoking now, they are likely to tell you that they never imagined that they could get hooked. They probably only wanted to have a feel, until they became addicted. According to the Department of Health and Human Services, it is estimated that each day approximately 2,100 youth and young adults who are occasional smokers become daily smokers. This is why it's better for you not to attempt smoking at all.

But, then, much more than addiction are far greater sources of concern that you really should be worried about. Here is a scary list as provided by the World Health Organization:

• Among young people, the short-term health consequences of smoking include respiratory and non-respiratory effects, addiction to nicotine, and the associated risk of other drug use. Long-term health consequences of youth smoking are reinforced by the fact that most young people who smoke regularly continue to smoke throughout adulthood. Cigarette smokers have a lower level of lung function than those persons who have never smoked. Smoking reduces the rate of lung growth.

- In adults, cigarette smoking causes heart disease and stroke. Studies have shown that early signs of these diseases can be found in adolescents who smoke.

- Smoking hurts young people's physical fitness in terms of both performance and endurance—even among young people trained in competitive running. On average, someone who smokes a pack or more of cigarettes each day lives 7 years less than someone who never smoked.

- The resting heart rates of young adult smokers are two to three beats per minute faster than nonsmokers.

- Smoking at an early age increases the risk of lung cancer. For most smoking-related cancers, the risk rises as the individual continues to smoke.

- Teenage smokers suffer from shortness of breath almost three times as often as teens who don't smoke, and produce phlegm more than twice as often as teens who don't smoke.

- Teenage smokers are more likely to have seen a doctor

or other health professionals for an emotional or psychological complaint.

- Teens who smoke are three times more likely than nonsmokers to use alcohol, eight times more likely to use marijuana, and times more likely to use cocaine. Smoking is associated with a host of other risky behaviors, such as fighting and engaging in unprotected sex.

Of course, you may think that e-cigarettes are safer than regular cigarettes because they don't contain tobacco. But the other ingredients in them are dangerous too. In fact, there are reports of serious lung damage and even death among people who use e-cigarettes. So, health experts strongly warn against using them.

I'm sure you have gotten a better picture now that smoking is not as "cool" as it appears. Please, stay away!

10

WHY SHOULD I DO EXERCISE?

Today's digital world presents teenagers with lots of entertainment and amusement options. We are in the days of realistic and futuristic video games. There is free Wi-Fi almost everywhere to surf the Internet and explore diverse social media platforms. There are also abundant cable channels with multitudes of interesting programs. All of these options are designed to keep you glued to your various gadgets all day. But you certainly don't want to do that because it is important that you create time for regular physical activity, also known as exercise.

You need regular exercise to live a healthy life and have a productive mind. This is why health experts, including the United States' Health and Human Services (HHS), have said that teenagers need at least 60 minutes of moderate to vigorous physical activity every day to remain healthy. And this is not something that happens on its own; it's something you must consciously determine to achieve because you will enjoy the benefits throughout your lifetime.

Don't be scared, though. Exercise or physical activity is not only about such vigorous activities as weightlifting, pushups, swimming, cycling or skipping ropes; it can also be something as simple as brisk walking, dancing or leg squats. Also, if you are very active in sporting activities during the week, chances are that you are getting enough amount of exercise already. Other activities you can engage in include in-line skating, skateboarding, shooting hoops in the driveway, riding a bicycle, walking a dog, mowing the lawn or raking leaves.

Whatever your choice is, you can be sure that adding as little as 45 minutes of moderate and intense physical activity to your day will not only help you stay fit and strong, but it will also help you to avoid diseases and health challenges like depression, diabetes, cardiovascular disease, and several types of cancer, particularly colon and breast cancers. Daily exercise can also help you reduce stress, brighten your mood, control your weight, sleep better, and sharpen your brain functioning.

By implication, therefore, daily exercise strengthens every part of your body, as well as your mind. It causes your body to produce chemicals that can help you to feel good. Remember also that all these are in addition to the fact that exercise can help you look better. Since exercise helps you to burn more calories, you naturally look and feel more energetic than those who don't exercise. Even if you currently have issues with your weight, exercise can help you lose weight and lower the risk of some diseases that come with being overweight.

One other benefit of exercise that you must know is that it will help you to age well. This means that even if you don't consider exercise or the lack of it as having any effect on your body now, you should be aware that it affects the way you age. For example, since exercise strengthens your bones and joints, it will be easier for your body to fight off diseases that cause weakening of bones and joints as you age.

All of these positive effects that exercise has on your body equally reflect on your mental health. With a fit, strong and well-toned body, your self-confidence is boosted, as well as your body image. This contributes significantly to your mood and attitude.

In a nutshell, exercise can:

- Help you maintain a healthy weight and reduce your chances of becoming overweight.

- Cut down your risk of developing heart diseases, diabetes and hypertension.

- Reduce your risk of getting cancers.

- Improve your mood, attitude and brainpower.

- Ensure your bones and joints stay strong for many years.

- Help you maintain your independence, well into your later years.

- Reduce symptoms of depression and anxiety.

- Lower your chances of heart disease.

- Manage chronic conditions like arthritis by helping with things like joint swelling, pain, and muscle strength.

- Help with your balance, so you're less likely to fall and break your bones.

In exercising, experts recommend that you should try to include a combination of aerobic activities (such as swimming or walking), strength training (such as sit-ups or weight training) and flexibility training (such as yoga or stretching). You must be careful, though, not to engage in exercise to the point of suffering sprains, fractures or other injuries.

11

WHY CAN'T I HAVE SEX NOW?

These days, sex is glamorized everywhere. In movies, television shows, advertisements, bestselling books, music videos and even in many so-called religious houses. Everywhere you turn, your senses are bombarded with the sights and sounds of sex. So, you cannot entirely avoid the pressure to think that it is the normal thing to do or that you are weird or missing out if you are not doing it. Even worse is that teenage and premarital sex is often celebrated in the media as harmless fun and a major proof of love, so much that many boys and girls today assume that the most realistic way to show their love for someone is to have sex with them.

In fact, some years back when a class teacher gave her pupils an assignment to define love, she was horrified at many of what she read. Most of what she read reflected a totally twisted perception of love. One of the definitions, from a five-year-old, read, "Love is when a boy meets a girl and they smile at each other, hold each other's hands and go into a room." Her understanding had apparently been driven by what she had been watching in movies and seeing around her.

It is not surprising therefore that many teenagers now think that having sex is what makes them cool or gives them a sense of belonging. Yet, the truth is that whichever way you look at it – physical, psychological, emotional or spiritual – teenage sex is merely an expressway to several problems, heartaches, sorrows and regrets. Yes, teenage sex can seem to be fun at first, but the painful consequences eventually overshadow whatever "fun" or enjoyment that may have been experienced.

Now, don't get me wrong. Sex in itself isn't bad. It is a beautiful act created by God to be enjoyed as one of the blessings of marriage. So, basically sex is meant to be enjoyed within the bond of marriage – that is, between two legally married people. Any other form of sex is an abuse of God's creation. And as you know, when something is abused or misused there are always repercussions. So it is with teenage sex.

The first problem of teenage sex is the feeling of guilt and loss of innocence. In fact, it comes with the worst hangover you can ever imagine. It is similar to what happened to Adam and Eve in the Garden of Eden. Of course, both Satan and the sensory perceptions of the man and the woman made it seem like eating the forbidden fruit was the best thing that could ever happen to them. Yet, as soon as they ate it, rather than the incredible feelings of delight and satisfaction they thought they would have, what happened was that "the eyes of both of them were opened, and they knew that they were naked…" (Genesis 3:7).

This is what happens as soon as you give in to pressure to indulge in premarital sex. Your eyes become open – not to anything glorious, but to feelings of shame, guilt and inadequacy. You feel you have lost something that can never be regained.

See, don't be fooled by what the media present to you or what your peers are saying. They may be making it seem like you are missing so much fun. But this is a mere bait to get you too to join the swelling throng of people who have been trapped by the intoxication of immoral sex. The truth is that, many teenagers who indulge in sex actually wish they could turn back the hands of time and return to the days when they do not have to deal with the burden of guilt and the feeling of being dirty and unworthy that comes with teenage sex.

Bear in mind that, in these your teenage years, your body is going through a period in which your hormones are raging and your body is rapidly developing. Hence, this can be a very confusing time to you. Your body may be sending signals to you that will make you feel like you are ready to have sex, which is a natural thing. But you should not only listen to what your body is telling you. Your beliefs, morals and values should be your guiding force during this time.

You should never give in to peer pressure about sexual activity.

Another thing is you should know is that once you allow your bodily urges and the pressures from around to make you start having sex, then it becomes very difficult for you to do without it. Note this carefully. Teenage sex is about the most addictive and destructive drug you can ever try. Once you begin, there's no telling where or how you'll end up because your body keeps demanding for more. You literally set your body on fire and this affects you emotionally and psychologically. You spend the bulk of your time thinking of it and your studies and other important areas of your life could be severely affected.

The third issue you should consider is that by engaging in teen sex, you cheapen and debase yourself to the other person and you give them the impression that you cannot discipline yourself or control your passions. Your worth before them immediately diminishes, as they have seen all about you and may even reduce you to a mere sex object who has no other significant value. Naturally, they no longer respect or appreciate you as they used to and you soon start getting boring to them. This is why you'll find that most teenage relationships involving sex only last for a while. This is also why teenage sex easily leads to depressive behaviors because with the diminished respect for you come all sorts of degrading tendencies and attitudes that were not there initially.

In the worst cases, the uncontrolled cravings that come with teenage sex have led many to having unwanted pregnancies and thus becoming accidental fathers and mothers. This not only places additional burdens on them but has actually derailed the dreams and destinies of many. Some try to commit abortion to hide their shame but this not only leaves them with a greater guilt of having committed murder, but there are also actually cases where things go wrong and damages occur to the reproductive system or there is loss of life. Even in cases of those who go ahead to have the unwanted child, severe complications sometimes arise because the body is not fully prepared for childbearing. There are also greater risks of sexually transmitted diseases, some of which can be very difficult to cure or could prove deadly.

Worst of all is the risk of facing God's judgment eventually. God has warned against fornication and all forms of premarital sex. And you will do yourself a lot of good and avoid sorrows and regrets by taking this warning seriously. Regardless of how rampant teenage sex has become, God's warning remains unchanged and His judgment is certain to come, one way or the other. "*Marriage is honorable* among all, and the bed undefiled; but fornicators and adulterers God will judge" (Hebrews 13:4).

All of these considerations must make you develop strength of character to reject the pressure of premarital sex. You will help yourself greatly by avoiding shows, movies, music, people and places that glamorize sex and stir immoral feelings and urges within you to indulge in it. And this advice from a counselor is particularly helpful, "If someone tries to coax you into sex by saying, "If you love me, you'll do this," firmly reply, "If you love *me*, you won't ask!"

Here are a couple things that you should consider doing as a teen if you feel pressured to have sex:

1. Talk to someone you trust, such as your parents, counselor, teacher, pastor or family doctor.

2. Pay attention to your feelings. Take a step back and really think about the consequences and risks associated with having pre-marital sex. Ask yourself whether it is the right thing to do. Think about the various consequences, as outlined above.

Consciously choosing not to have sex before marriage is okay. Many young people make the choice to wait. This is a decision that I can assure you is the safest!

12

WHY CAN'T I GET PREGNANT OR IMPREGNATE SOMEONE NOW?

Pregnancy is a good thing. If it wasn't for pregnancy, you and I would not be here. It is the process the creator has put in place to populate the earth. Again, the process is good, very good and the joy of having a new born baby in your hands is indeed a great feeling. The only problem now is the timing. You see, there is an appropriate time for everything on earth. And, certainly, now is not a good time for you to get pregnant or impregnate someone.

Why is this so? Well, in the first place, you shouldn't even be having sex at your age. There are more important engagements that should occupy your time and mind at this time. This is the time for you to start getting mentally, physically, socially and spiritually for your future and fulfillment of your destiny. In fact, more than any other thing else, a significant portion of your time should be spent acquiring knowledge and getting sound education.

The dangers and distractions of teenage sex are troubles you want to do everything possible to avoid.

But then, it is possible you have seen people become fathers and mothers and cradling their newborns. Maybe this fascinates you and you feel, "why can't I do just that? I love babies!" As I've noted at the beginning, this feeling is good but the timing is not. Especially as a teenage girl, you are not biologically or physically ready for pregnancy. You will pose a challenge to the medical profession and a major risk to yourself because your body is just not ready for that. Even worse is that you could expose the child to birth defects and a very difficult life afterwards.

Since your body itself is still developing, it will be difficult for it to provide the needed nutrition and care that the baby needs. And of course, there is also the emotional and psychological maturity that pregnancy requires. See, it may seem cool when you see cute pregnant women or cuddly little babies, but the truth is, pregnancy is no fun or child's play, especially in the early months. Your body will go through changes that you may not be ready to handle. In fact, it could freak you out. You'll have to deal with morning sickness, stretch marks, intense hormones, weight gain and other issues.

The growing fetus in your womb too may suffer some unpleasant experiences. First of all, since you may not be immediately aware of the early signs of pregnancy, you may deny the fetus the essential medical care it needs within the early months for proper development. This denial of care is also more likely if your parents refuse to support you. And of course, you will hardly see a parent who will not be angry or disappointed in you and in themselves for your getting pregnant as a teenager. They will be sad and angry that their efforts and dreams for you will be wasted; and they will be disappointed as they would keep wondering where and how they had failed as parents. With this state of mind, it will be hard for your parents to guide and support you in getting prenatal care which should help to prevent problems for you and the child.

The various biological, social, emotional and psychological challenges that come with teenage pregnancy could also expose you to high blood pressure. In fact, it has been variously proven that pregnant teens have a higher risk of getting high blood pressure – called pregnancy-induced hypertension – than women who get pregnant when they are older. Since hypertension often proves to be the gateway to more severe health issues that could sometimes prove fatal, you may want to take medications to control the symptoms. Unfortunately, this also can prove to be risky because such medications can have frightening effects on the baby.

Another reality that should put you off pregnancy now is that the chances of premature birth are high in teenage pregnancies. Premature birth refers to the situation in which pregnancy does not last the full pregnancy term of 40 weeks. Many teenage mothers usually experience labor as early as in the 37th week, which may or may not be stopped with medications. In some cases, the baby has to be delivered early because of posed health risks to mother and the infant. Things could get worse because a premature birth could come with other medical complications, such as respiratory and digestive problems for the baby.

Besides, whether a teenage pregnancy lasts the full pregnancy term or not, there will also be concerns for a safe delivery. Because the body is often not fully ready at this time for the rigors of delivery, it is often a difficult time for everyone involved. In fact, the lives of both the mother and child are usually at stake. According to the World Health Organization (WHO), "Adolescent pregnancy remains a major contributor to maternal and child mortality, and to intergenerational cycles of ill-health and poverty. Pregnancy and childbirth complications are the leading cause of death among 15 to 19 year-old girls globally."

Again, even when there is a safe delivery, there are still more issues to worry about. Here is what WHO has to say on this: "Babies born to mothers under 20 years of age face higher risks of low birth weight, preterm delivery, and severe neonatal conditions Newborns born to adolescent mothers are also at greater risk of having low birth weight, with long-term potential effects. In some settings, rapid repeat pregnancy is a concern for young mothers, which presents further risks for both the mother and child."

You should also know that there is something called

"postpartum depression" – which typically develops within 4 to 6 weeks after giving birth and involves severe mood swings, exhaustion, and a sense of hopelessness. This condition can affect women of all ages, but it has been medically proven that the rate is higher in teenage mothers in comparison with other mothers. This is to be expected as teens are often unprepared for the realities involved in parenting an infant. Often, complex relationships and financial burden, combined with balancing school and parenting, are stressful and can put both you and the newborn at risk.

But it is not only teenage mothers who have problems to contend with. If you impregnate someone as a teenage boy, you should know that you are not only putting the girl at risk of all the dangers mentioned above, but you will also be exposing yourself to a life of restlessness, distress and depression. You may have to stop your education to get a job that will make you provide for your baby and the mother.

Considering all these troubles associated with teenage parenthood, I will advise that you engage more in things that will make you capable and sufficient enough to care for the baby or babies you plan to have in future. These include your education, developing your talents and potentials, and getting or creating jobs.

13

WHY CAN'T I EAT SNACKS FOR BREAKFAST?

The first thing you should know is that breakfast is your most important meal of the day. This is basically because it serves the dual purpose of refueling your body after a long night of rest and other bodily functions, while also preparing you for the various activities you have ahead in the day. This means that without eating a good breakfast, you won't have the energy you need to be productively active and creative throughout the day.

A good breakfast also makes you more mentally alert and receptive to learning. You will find it easier to concentrate, recall and solve problems. Essentially, with a good breakfast, you are well-positioned to perform better in school and in all other activities of the day. Added to this renewed energy and mental focus is an enhanced mood. Healthy breakfasts have been proven to make people feel less tired, restless, or irritable.

A good breakfast will also help you in maintaining a healthy weight. It does this in two ways. One is by helping to trigger your body's metabolism – the process by which your body converts the fuel in food to energy. And once the metabolism starts, your body starts burning calories and thus preventing excess storage of fat in your body. The second way breakfast helps you to maintain a healthy weight is that it prevents you from trying to make up for your skipped breakfast with high-calorie snacks or trying to overeat later in the day. It has indeed been confirmed that people who don't eat breakfast often consume more calories throughout the day and are more likely to be overweight. That's because someone who skips breakfast is likely to get famished before lunchtime and snack on high-calorie foods or overeat at lunch.

With this very important role that breakfast plays in making you have an awesome day, you can now easily understand why your parents would insist on you having a healthy and wholesome diet in the morning. Snacks are not meals; they are primarily meant to be taken in-between meals, especially before lunch or dinner, but certainly not as breakfast. Snacks are not satisfying and thus do not contain the wholesome energy content needed to sustain your activities within those critical early hours of the morning.

A healthy breakfast needs to have a balance of the different classes of food, especially carbohydrates, protein and fat, to keep your energy levels steady all morning. Of course, you may feel a bit full and somewhat satisfied after taking a snack for breakfast, but experience has shown that though snacks briefly satisfy hunger and promote feelings of fullness, the fact that they do not have the right balance of nutrients will soon cause you to start feeling hungry again. And your craving for more food will certainly result in an increased calorie intake for the day, which automatically opens the door for obesity.

Findings have also shown that most of the widely consumed snack foods are high in refined carbohydrates or added sugar and low in nutritional value. This naturally poses an increased risk of developing heart disease and increased cholesterol levels. On the other hand, choosing breakfast foods that are rich in whole grains, fiber, and protein, while low in added sugar, will boost your attention span, concentration, and memory, as well as your energy level.

On the whole, teenagers who eat breakfast are more likely to get fiber, calcium, and other important nutrients. They also tend to keep their weight under control, have lower blood cholesterol levels and fewer absences from school, and make fewer trips to the school nurse with stomach complaints related to hunger.

PART 4

ABOUT YOUR EDUCATION

14

WHY DO I HAVE TO GO TO SCHOOL?

Well, first of all, you must understand that the feeling behind this question is pretty normal. Even adults who go to work sometimes don't feel like it, and they wonder if there could be an alternative. Yeah, that is the truth. I mean, who doesn't like just curling up in bed for as long as possible, hanging out with friends, watching movies, listening to trending music, playing games, scouring the Internet, going on picnics and generally enjoying life? But the problem is that choosing to live that way will not only bring poverty but also setbacks and lack of fulfilment in every area of life.

Okay, back to the school issue. There are three important benefits you get from attending school. These benefits have to do with **what** you get, **how** you get it and **where** you get it. You go to school to get what is known as education. Why do you need this? First, education helps to unlock the power for possibilities that is within you. You see, you were born to be great. God, who made you, has put some amazing abilities in you, which you may not fully discover, develop or put into good use without getting an education. This is why most of the greatest men and women who ever lived and changed the world for better were people who received good education.

Education makes you to learn different skills. Depending on the type of school you attend, education generally equips you with academic skills, vocational skills and life skills. Academic skills refer to such skills as reading, writing, drawing and doing arithmetic. Vocational skills have to do with practical skills that prepare you for work in a specific trade, craft, or profession. They are skills that help you to gain mastery as a technician or artisan - such that, by the time you graduate, you would be ready to become an entrepreneur, with the ability to manage your own business or company. Life skills or "soft skills" are such that help you to apply both the theoretical and the practical knowledge you acquire in school to real world problems and situations. They are skills that help you to demonstrate sound judgment in making decisions, as well as to develop good habits that will enhance your wellbeing, relationships and overall success in life.

Now, take some time to consider how many wonderful things you have learned in school from your preschool years till now. These things have contributed to your having a better view of life and being able to do a number of tasks, as well as relating well with others. Even more interesting is that the more education you get, the better you become at doing things well, positively influencing others and changing the world around you for good.

Also, since the education you get in school covers different subjects, issues and skills, this makes you to have a better understanding and mastery of your environment. Without this knowledge and understanding, there is a lot you will be ignorant of and confused about. This not only makes you prone to making mistakes, but also being very limited in your contribution to the world around you.

Most importantly, education helps to expand and enrich your mind. You think deeper and become more creative. It was Oliver Wendell Holmes Jnr., former associate Justice of the Supreme Court, who once said, "A man's mind, stretched by new ideas, may never return to its original dimensions." This means that getting quality education helps you to do things you never would have thought yourself capable of doing. This stimulates you to better appreciate the world around you, while at the same time preparing you to have a rewarding career in the nearest future. The truth is that most employers need to have proofs that you have been trained and prepared to excel in whatever role you are being assigned. Only your level of education, backed by the necessary certification and demonstration of competence, can immediately provide this proof.

But, of course, you may say that you could still get an education without necessarily being in the classroom. And that brings us to the "where" part of the benefits of attending school. The school environment functions in such a way as to not only stimulate your desire to learn but to make you understand the things you learn better. You see, the way you receive education in a school environment is quite different from what happens outside of it. Going to school gives you the opportunity to meet other young folks like you, who you can easily interact, socialize and make friends with.

Within the school environment, you engage in a lot of activities together and generally have a great time with nearly no dull moment. In fact, some of the best memories you will cherish for a lifetime are likely to come from the moments you share together with your school mates.

Additionally, being in school gives you the opportunity to learn from others, since each of your peers has his or her special abilities and interesting characteristics. Note also that school is not all about reading books and listening to teachers all day. There are also opportunities to indulge in your favorite hobbies and games with your peers who have same interest as you.

Most schools have trained and professional educators who will teach and guide you, based on principles and guidelines prepared by experts in child education, psychology and the likes. You will find most of these educators to be very kind and supportive. They will try as much as possible to familiarize themselves with you, to understand your educational needs and how best to meet them. They also initiate activities that are specially designed not only to stimulate your brain and mind, but also to keep you active and productive.

You have to go school therefore to learn, discover yourself, develop your potentials, socialize, have fun and prepare for a beautiful future – all in a safe and conducive environment.

15

WHY DO I HAVE TO DO MY HOMEWORK?

Homework is school work given to students to be done at home. It usually consists of a set of tasks assigned by your teachers for you to complete outside of the classroom. It could be for you to read up a passage, solve some mathematical problems, do some drawing and other practical works, or practice some skills.

But then, whichever form it takes, homework can be a pain – except you understand its purpose and benefits. I mean, it ordinarily doesn't seem fair that what is meant for school should be taken home. Why should school work not remain in school? Why should the little time you have at home after school to relax, amuse yourself and hang out with friends be taken over or even shortened by more school work?

I'm sure, however, that you will come to love and appreciate the homework given to you by your teachers once you understand that it is mostly for your own benefit. For instance, in 2006, a group of researchers conducted a study titled, *"Does Homework Improve Academic Achievement?"* What they found will be of interest to you. According to them, "Among teenagers, students who spend somewhat more time on homework generally have higher grades, and somewhat higher test scores than students who spend less time on homework."

There are other proofs from individual students and those who have taken time to study the impact of homework on students' performance that will convince you to take your homework seriously. Homework has been proven to significantly improve students' knowledge and understanding of what they are taught in class. This is especially so as homework is often based on situations outside of what you must have been exposed to in class. So, it helps you to think deeper and more practically. It also helps you to study and prepare in advance for more difficult topics that will be taught later.

What this means is that doing your homework helps to sharpen your intellect, as you are able to work independently without your teacher's input. It also helps you to manage your time and use it more productively because you are able to set your priorities right. Since you are likely to get homework from different subjects, you are able to allocate time to each, and ensure that you complete all before the deadlines. This, in a way, teaches you both discipline and responsibility – two essential ingredients for success in all areas of life. It also teaches you perseverance because you sometimes have to make several attempts, with a lot of thinking and practice, before you are able to solve some of the assignments you are given.

Also, in doing your homework, you are able to go over what you have done in class once more, which gives you a better understanding of what you have been taught. And you know what? As you gain this further understanding, in addition to your being able to successfully complete your homework, you become a much more confident student and your self-esteem receives consistent boost.

Interestingly, you are not the only one who benefits when you take your homework seriously. Both your teachers and your parents benefit as well, which will in turn bring added benefits to you. For instance, how you tackle some of the tasks you are given helps your teacher to know how much you understand what you have been taught. It will help them to know areas where you need further help, as well as areas they also need to improve upon, both in the content and the pattern of their teaching.

For your parents, your homework – which may sometimes require their assistance – helps them to have an idea of what you are being taught in school. And in the instances that they have to guide you, not only does it strengthen the bond between you and your parents (and even siblings), but it will also let them know when they need to call your teachers to discuss areas of concern or point out steps that can be taken to improve your overall performance.

In summary therefore, aside from helping to improve your use of time, homework makes you an active participant in your learning process because it helps you to develop important problem-solving skills.

16

WHY SHOULD I DO HOUSEHOLD CHORES?

None can deny that you certainly do have a lot to deal with already, especially with the demands of school work and other extra-curricular activities. But the thing is, as important as these engagements are, you cannot have a balanced life without learning to help around the house. Household chores are those activities that members of the family engage in within and around the house to ensure that the family is running smoothly and that the home environment is kept tidy.

Household chores are not only meant for adults. Everyone - especially teenagers who are at the period of transiting from the childhood years that had very limited responsibilities to the adulthood years with loads of responsibilities – have important roles to play. Some of the duties you can engage in, as recommended by the American Academy of Pediatrics, include, putting away your belongings, doing the laundry, folding and putting away clean clothes, vacuuming, sweeping, dusting, setting the table for meals, clearing the table after meals, washing and putting away the dishes, feeding and walking family pets, cleaning birdcages and litter boxes, mopping floors, scrubbing the sink, toilet, bathtub and shower stall, preparing your own lunches for school,   cooking dinner one night a week, doing yardwork and washing the family car.

Even when housekeepers or domestic staff are employed in the family, it is still important for you as a teenager to be involved in lending a helping hand – not just for the family as a whole, but for yourself in particular. Experience has shown that being involved in household chores comes with loads of benefits. The most important of this is that it teaches you responsibility, self-reliance and survival skills.

You see, you are young now, but you are growing into an adult who will sooner or later have to live independently. If you are not used to home-keeping now, it will be much more difficult then. But then, even as a teenager, it is not every time you will live at home or with your parents. When you go to college, for example, how do you do basic chores and tidy up your room? It is usually very saddening and embarrassing to see college students who cannot do such basic chores as using the washing machine, using a vacuum cleaner, making a bed or changing the sheets – all because they have been so used to having everything done for them. But if you start doing the chores when you are at home, not only would it soon become a part of you, but you would have also had your mistakes corrected and would have mastered most of the activities before leaving home.

Joining in household chores also makes the work easy for others. If you can, for instance, begin with the principle of cleaning up after yourself or dealing with every mess you make, you will find that your parents and siblings would have fewer things to worry about when doing chores. Not only that, as you join others in helping around the house, it helps in creating special moments for you and other members of your family to bond. And you also enjoy the beauty and goodness of teamwork.

Doing household chores will also help you to appreciate the good efforts of others – your parents, domestic helps and siblings – in keeping your home tidy at all times. In fact, it is a good way of letting your parents know how much you cherish their efforts towards meeting your needs and making you happy. And you can be sure that once you know that you will be involved in clearing up whatever mess is made in the house, you will also be more careful in the way you handle things.

Being assigned chores in the house is also a way of your parents showing that they trust you enough to be competent and responsible. And, so, you should respect, rather than resent them for making such a decision. Ultimately, with your parents constantly expressing confidence in your ability to carry out chores, as well your success at executing most of these chores and getting the rewards thereafter, you will experience a huge surge in your self-esteem and gradually develop a strong sense of work ethic.

Generally, research and experience have shown that teenagers who do have a set of household chores have higher self-esteem, are more responsible, and are better able to deal with frustration and delay gratification, all of which contribute to greater success in school and later in work and family life.

17

WHY AM I BEING DISCIPLINED?

Discipline or punishment is part of the measures that all loving parents take to remind their children that they love them and want them to keep to family rules, respect boundaries and avoid behaviors that can cause them harm. Punishment is usually applied when you have committed some serious misdeed or repeatedly disobeyed instructions.

For you, as a teenager, this punishment is most likely to come in form of deprivation – which involves your parents temporarily taking away a privilege or something of value from you. Your parents may prevent you from using a gadget or they may refuse to pay for certain services that you should have enjoyed. They may also "ground" you by preventing you from visiting certain friends or going for some events.

Now, one thing you have to understand is that your parents don't really enjoy punishing you or making you go through the discomforts of discipline. They love you too much for that. But, then, they also know that you cannot grow to become a responsible adult who takes rules seriously and considers the feelings of others without them sometimes using this tough approach. Even the Holy Scripture says, "At the time, discipline isn't much fun. It always feels like it's going against the grain. Later, of course, it pays off handsomely…" (Hebrews 12:11, MSG)

So, why do your parents punish you? They do so to let you know that actions have consequences. More specifically, they want you to know that choosing to make wrong choices could bring unpleasant outcomes. Imagine that you consistently break family rules and your parents just laugh it off. You would consider it normal to break rules and will find it hard to exercise self-control and good judgment in most other areas of your life. Therefore, punishment helps you to manage your emotions and respect rules.

Your parents also punish you to show they really care about you. If they didn't care about you, they wouldn't bother going through the stress of making you abide by rules or change your behavior. If they didn't believe you could amount to something in life, why bother trying to keep you from bad behavior or self-harm? Here again is what the Holy Scripture says, "For the Lord disciplines those he loves, and he punishes each one he accepts as his child. As you endure this divine discipline, remember that God is treating you as his own children. Who ever heard of a child who is never disciplined by its father? If God doesn't discipline you as he does all of his children, it means that you are illegitimate and are not really his children at all" (Hebrews 12:6-8). This is what happens with our earthly parents too.

Your parents also punish you to keep you safe. They don't want you to continue with habits and behaviors that can ultimately harm you or others, or mar your chances of becoming a successful person in life. And guess what? Whether you know it or not, your parents' seeming strict involvement in your life ultimately creates in you a very high level of confidence and esteem, knowing that you're not just abandoned to navigate life on your own.

A recent study discovered that young men with high self-esteem, as well as those with low self-esteem shared some common childhood influences. One, the high-esteem group was clearly more loved and appreciated at home than the low-esteem group. Two, The high-esteem group came from homes where parents had been significantly stricter in their approach to discipline. By contrast, the parents of the low-esteem group had created insecurity and dependence through their permissiveness. Their children were more likely to feel that the rules were not enforced because no one cared enough to get involved. Three, the homes of the high-esteem group were also characterized by democracy and openness. Once the boundaries were established, there was freedom for individual personalities to grow and develop. So, the overall atmosphere was marked by acceptance and emotional safety.

Now you know better why your parents can't let you have your way all the time. You are just so precious to them. However, it is also important for you to know that there is a clear difference between acceptable discipline (punishment) and gross abuse. Discipline, as we have seen, so far, stems from love. Consequently, what drives its expression and guides its application is genuine concern for your wellbeing. For this reason, discipline is not applied in anger and frustration or with the intention to inflict physical or psychological harm.

This explanation should help you to know when your parents or whoever is trying to discipline you begins to cross the line of abuse. According to relevant authorities in child protection, punishment becomes abusive when:

- It involves physical injury, including bruising, broken skin, swelling or a situation that requires medical attention.

- It is meant to instill fear in you, rather than to educate you.

- Your parents or anyone else meting out the punishment loses control.

- Punitive measures are inappropriate for your age.

- It involves or comes from their unreasonable demands or expectations from you.

-

- It involves hostility, aggression, cruelty or sadistic behavior.

If you experience any of the above, especially on continuous basis, then you may need to speak with a counselor or reach out to a child protective services agency close to you for support.

18

WHY DO I NEED TO HAVE GOOD MANNERS?

Some time ago, a young man on a train got into a serious and aggressive argument with a much older man, which eventually led to some very serious consequences. What happened was that the young man was scheduled to be at a job interview and he was almost late. In his haste to get on the train, he bumped into the older man who was close to the doorway. The older man was angry, but the young man felt his anger was pointless, since he had simply been at the wrong place at the wrong time. They got into a more heated argument that might have turned physical if the other passengers hadn't intervened.

When the young man got to the interview venue, he was directed to a waiting room. After some minutes, he was called to face the interview panel. To his dismay, the man on the train was the head of the panel. Of course, you can easily guess the outcome of that interview. And I'm sure you'll agree that things might have taken a different turn, if the young man had just said something as simple as "sorry" to the older man. This is an example of the importance of having good manners.

Having good manners or courtesy means showing polite behavior and proper conduct. It encompasses being kind, generous, compassionate and socially aware. It is a basic attribute of all truly civilized people. In fact, it is the number one proof of how enlightened, intelligent and thoughtful you are. Moreover, it reflects good upbringing, respect and consideration for others and is also a way of showing others how you expect them to treat you. Most importantly, as the opening story shows, it can be a determinant of what opportunities you get and how far you can go in life.

It is especially important to emphasize the importance of showing good manners, considering the massive damage that modern technological devices are doing to the mannerisms of many people, especially teenagers. It is not uncommon these days for an elderly person or someone in a leadership position to walk into a room or class and find nearly all the teenagers with their faces glued to their gadgets and none willing to acknowledge the presence of the individual, show any form of respect or respond to greetings. Even when such acknowledgement is done, it is either done without making eye contact or with a muffled expression. This has created many avoidable problems for a teeming number of teenagers.

Examples of good manners or courteous behavior include saying "please" and "thank you"; sincerely apologizing when you've done something wrong; observing table etiquette; not interrupting when someone is talking; not rushing to be first in line; helping the elderly, the weak, the sick and the disabled; responding when spoken to; respecting the privacy of others; not saying rude things to others; following rules; not texting or using the Internet when talking to people face-to-face; muting or switching off your phone when having important meetings or conversation; covering your mouth when you sneeze or cough; and so on.

Three out of the above examples of good manners require particular attention, especially for teenagers. These include saying "please" or "excuse me" (taking permission), saying "thank you" (appreciating other people's efforts and kindness) and saying "sorry" (apologizing when you've done something wrong). These three expressions are said to be magical because of the amazing effects they can have on your relationships with others.

It is important to say "please" when you are making a request or taking permission – whether you are addressing your parents or peers. Doing so is both a sign of respect and a way of showing that you are not taking advantage of others or taking them for granted. Without saying "please", most of your requests will sound like demands and whoever you're talking to would be less motivated to grant your request.

Saying "thank you" is a way of showing that you appreciate the efforts and gestures of others towards you. It shows that you understand that it must have cost them something – time, energy, money or anything else – to do whatever they have done for you. This attitude of gratitude will not only make your benefactor happy, but it also make them more willing to keep being nice to you. This is why Jacques Maritain says, "Gratitude is the most exquisite form of courtesy." The more you are thankful for every little thing done for your benefit, the more of such gestures you will receive.

Also, when you acknowledge your mistakes and apologize for any wrong done to others knowingly or unknowingly, it helps to soothe and calm the person you have hurt and makes them feel better about themselves. It also tells a lot about your great personality, humility and thoughtfulness. It shows that you respect the feelings of others and place much value on your relationship with them. Above all, it shows that you are willing to accept responsibility for your faults, learn from them and prevent them from happening again.

So, dear friend, make it a habit to practice good manners always. More importantly, use the "magical words" as often as you can, and you will be amazed at the "magical" benefits that they will daily attract to you.

19

WHY DO I HAVE TO SAVE MY MONEY?

This is an interesting question that most young people ask because, come to think of it, saving doesn't sound like something meant for the young. It seems more like what adults should be bothering about. After all, they are the ones handling the financial budgeting, planning and spending for the family. And for whatever little money an average teenager makes, whether from a job or regular allowance, there is usually a long list of fun things to buy and enjoy.

But then, we still must return to the basic reality that a teenager is just a few years away from becoming a full blown adult. And isn't today the best time to prepare for tomorrow? Certainly. So, if you want to master the secrets of making, managing and multiplying money, as well as planning and spending wisely, such that you're never in financial lack, then now is the time you must begin.

The reason many adults often have money problems is

because they didn't take the principle of saving money seriously from their younger years. This is one reason you must take this seriously because if you can develop the habit of saving and planning the way you spend money from now, it will prepare you for a secure future that will be void of financial worries and troubles.

It is particularly necessary for you as a teenager to know how to save because you are more prone to pressure to spend your money carelessly. As you are daily bombarded with advertisements that are demanding you to go for the latest fashion items, devices, applications and snacks, so also do you have peers who are ready to make you feel like a misfit if you do not go for these things. The result of which is often an endless cycle of buying and discarding.

"America Saves", an initiative of Consumer Federation of America, which encourages households to save money, shares the experience of a young man, Johnnie Lovett, which is very instructive for every teenager. Johnnie's parents had introduced him to the concepts of budgeting, saving, and money management in his teenage years. It was at a time when he was finding it difficult to balance his needs with his wants. According to him, "I found out I wasn't always able to buy the things I wanted." Fortunately for him, he took his parents' advice seriously and has never regretted doing so.

Addressing teenagers, Johnnie said, "As young adults, we don't realize how much money we have our hands on because we're constantly spending." Luckily for him, his parents had made it clear to him that "saving is a habit and it's essential to living." Consequently, he soon began to regularly save a little portion of his every income before making a list of his needs and budgeting for them. This helped him so much to successfully manage his expenses.

And guess what? Saving has so become a part of Johnnie's life that he's already putting some money aside to purchase a house as soon as he graduates from university. He says, "Owning a house is part of my long-term financial plan, so I'm putting aside money towards a down payment now."

But before you think that saving is such a huge task, here is Johnnie's advice, "The best way to save is to pick a goal amount, such as a percentage or dollar amount, and save that out of every paycheck. Stick to your goal, rather than trying to save an entire paycheck, which isn't realistic."

Learning to save now will certainly make you a master of your finances. It will make you live a more disciplined life, which, among other things, will help you in handling financial products such as credit cards, payday loans, and mobile phone contracts. It will help you set money goals and achieve them, as well as growing wealth. It will make you learn to live a life of independence and be a lender, rather than a borrower.

You can start now to save. If you are up to 18, begin by opening a savings account. If you're under 18, ask your parents to help you out. After that, start depositing as much as you can into the account. As you do this, you'll also be thinking of the various ways you can generate income so as to keep having a steady flow of money into the account. Also, learn to cut down on your expenses by looking for ways to cut costs and avoid buying things that are not so important.

As you keep to this habit of saving with consistency, determination and discipline, you will soon find yourself becoming like one of the wealthy folks you've always admired!

PART 5

ABOUT PEER PRESSURE

20

WHY SHOULD I RESIST PEER PRESSURE?

Peer pressure is the influence that your buddies try to enforce on your thinking and behavior. This influence can be direct or indirect. It is direct when your peers try to make you do certain things as a condition for you to fit in among them. It is indirect, when something seems like a general trend among your peers and it feels like being the odd person out if you don't join the trend.

Every teenager faces peer pressure because the tendency is stronger at this stage of life to base your worth on how much you are accepted and admired by your peers. Unfortunately, since most of the youths who form the influencing group are still ignorant about many issues of life and making right decisions, pressure coming from them is often negative. And this is where the challenge comes – how do you resist such a negative influence that is often aimed at making you rebel against authority, morality, decency and godliness?

Your number one defense against negative peer pressure is to always remind yourself that giving in to such influence will only make you lose yourself while trying to put on an identity being imposed on you by others. By yielding to negative pressure, in whichever form it comes, you end up losing your unique identity, focus and peace of mind. This is why someone said that "if you follow the crowd, you might get lost in it." Another said, "When you are saying yes to others, you're gradually saying no to yourself." The end result, of course, is often frustration.

Here is an interesting story to further explain this. Some years back, a man opened a fish stall in an outdoor market and placed a sign in front of it: "FRESH FISH SOLD HERE TODAY". Soon, a customer came and told him, "Your sign is too long. Take down the word "FRESH", everyone knows you won't sell fish that's not fresh!" "Okay," says the vendor, and he took down "FRESH".

Soon, another customer came and said, "Why do you need the word "TODAY"? When else could it be!" The vendor took down "TODAY". Still, another customer came and said "HERE! Where else? The vendor took down "HERE," the sign said "FISH SOLD". Another customer scoffed, "SOLD? Do you think anyone would think you are giving the fish away?" The vendor took down "SOLD" leaving only the word "FISH". "Why FISH?" another shopper asked. With a smell like this, do you even need a sign at all?" Finally, the man had nothing left of his sign and, needless to say, his business collapsed within a short time.

This is what happens when you allow yourself to be influenced against your convictions and the wise counsel of your parents and other authority figures around you. You should both be watchful enough to differentiate between helpful and harmful suggestions from your peers, as well as being bold enough to reject wrongful influence. Shannon L. Alder says, "Confidence is knowing who you are and not changing it a bit because of someone's version of reality is not your reality."

Your second defense is to be mindful of the people you associate with. It will be very difficult, if not totally impossible, for you to withstand negative peer pressure when you are often around other teenagers who drink, smoke, engage in immoral relationships, make dirty jokes, bully others, dress indecently or are unserious about their studies. In fact, the Bible puts it directly, "Do not be deceived: "Evil company corrupts good habits." (1 Corinthians 15:33). As if to confirm this, a study by researchers at Columbia University shows that kids are six times more likely to have had a drink if their friends often drink alcohol.

Your third source of defense is to get used to criticism. You cannot resist peer pressure if you are always worried about what others think of you or if you are always in need of others' approval to take decisions about your life. One truth you must realize is that you cannot avoid criticism if you want to amount to anything significant in life. Criticism is a vital ingredient of greatness. This is why it is said that "to avoid criticism, say nothing, do nothing, be nothing."

Every successful person who brought great changes to the world had moments that they had to endure criticism and pressures to give up on their beliefs and causes. If they had been too concerned about what people thought of them, you probably wouldn't be hearing about them today. So, don't be bothered if others taunt or tease you for being different from them. It's pretty normal. As Albert Einstein said, "Great spirits have always encountered violent opposition from mediocre minds."

Lastly, you must know that there are consequences in either choosing to allow or reject peer pressure. Your choice now will definitely affect your life and future for good or otherwise. Now is the time you must determine to develop the backbone to do what is right at all times.

21

WHY SHOULD I NOT BE OVERWHELMED BY MY MISTAKES?

During the 1961 Masters Tournament, legendary golfer, Arnold Palmer, made a very terrible mistake. He had only the final hole of the tournament left, and having had a one-stroke lead and had just hit a very powerful tee shot, he became conceited. One of his friends in the gallery motioned to him for a congratulatory handshake, which he accepted. And that was the beginning of failure for him. He lost focus, missed his next shot and lost the Masters.

Now, this is the most interesting part. Instead of allowing that mistake to crush him, Arnold turned it to a powerful force to propel him to greater wins. He became even more focused and determined than he had ever been. As he would later say, "You don't forget a mistake like that; you just learn from it and become determined that you will never do that again. I haven't in the 30 years since."

That's exactly what happens when you don't allow your mistakes to hold you down or define your worth. Mistakes only make you human – because everyone makes them. Mistakes don't make you a failure; they only come to make you wiser, smarter and stronger. As Steve Maraboli says, "We all make mistakes, have struggles, and even regret things in our past. But you are not your mistakes, you are not your struggles, and you are here NOW with the power to shape your day and your future."

This is the reason you must not allow yourself to be crippled by your mistakes. They form an essential part of the ingredients of your growth, maturity and expertise. You remember the popular response attributed to Thomas Edison, when he had repeatedly failed at an experiment and was asked why he wouldn't give up? He said that those earlier failed attempts had only revealed the wrong approaches to the invention he was working on. And with that, he could concentrate more on other approaches.

This is the same attitude you find in most other achievers in life. They don't see themselves as super humans, who cannot or must not make mistakes; rather, they are ever prepared to learn from their mistakes and get better. And you know what? This is actually the secret of their success. Because they are not bothered about making mistakes, they are never hesitant to make attempts. And because they keep making attempts, they keep winning and discovering what many who are fearful of making mistakes can't see.

So, first, don't see mistakes as markers of failure; see them as opportunities to learn. Be willing to admit it when you make one, and then determine not to repeat it. This way, you would have gained more knowledge and experience that will continue to prove useful to you. Second, don't waste your precious time regretting your mistakes. There's no point crying over spilled milk. And, of course, no amount of regret can undo whatever you may have done wrong. As Katherine Mansfield has rightly observed, "Regret is an appalling waste of energy, you can't build on it - it's only good for wallowing in."

So, what you do is look away from the doors that seem to have been closed by your mistakes and focus more on the many more doors of success and learning that have been opened to you. Here's Michael Jordan's experience, "I've missed more than 9000 shots in my career. I've lost almost 300 games. Twenty-six times I've been trusted to take the game winning shot and missed. I've failed over and over and over again in my life. And that is why I succeed."

What's the iconic basketball player saying here? That each of his mistakes and failures had only ended up teaching him vital lessons and secrets that turned him to the global champion he eventually became. That's what you too should determine to do with each of your mistakes. Let them spur you to be a better person; but be determined not to repeat them.

22

WHY CAN'T I HAVE A BOYFRIEND OR GIRLFRIEND NOW?

Recently, a young man raised this alarm online: "I am 21 and never had a girlfriend. Most of my friends are in a relationship. I feel kind of depressed and that I would never have a girlfriend. What should I do?"

I can clearly understand the feeling of this young man because it reflects the state of mind of many young men and women. For many teenagers, in particular, it seems quite strange and unthinkable that they shouldn't be in a romantic relationship. With a combination of pressure coming from the hormones that are raging in their developing bodies and the pressure coming from their peers, as well as the misleading messages from the media, most youngsters consider having a boyfriend or girlfriend as what determines their worth.

Indeed, a US-based National Longitudinal Study of Adolescent Health (Add Health), involving a representative sample of thousands of school children in Grades 7 to 12, found that over 80 per cent of those aged 14 years and older were or had been in a romantic relationship. So rampant is the relationship pressure among teenagers that there is hardly a conversation lasting for some minutes among them that the topic of who is dating who doesn't come up.

This is why it is not unusual to find teenagers getting worried that they have no boyfriend or girlfriend. Yet, for the very few who make up their minds to not be influenced by both internal and external pressures to get into a relationship, they sooner or later come to understand that they have indeed made the right choice and have avoided lots of sorrows and snares by choosing to be "odd". And I do earnestly hope that you too will, like the biblical "Hebrew children", choose to be among these few wise ones who choose to remain strong and steadfast when multitudes around them are falling.

Why did I say that? You see, contrary to the false impressions that your peers, the media and the society, as a whole, tend to give about teenage romantic relationships, it is actually filled with many dangers. As you will discover, the gains that those who are involved in such relationships seem to enjoy are not worth the troubles, trauma and frustrations that come with it.

What you should understand, first of all, is that romantic relationships involve much more than mutual attraction and stolen pleasures. There is usually a heavy demand on your time, emotion, attention and composure. Even for adults, it is quite demanding; so you can imagine what it is like for teenagers who are yet to figure out so many things about life.

The teenage years are characterized by amazing transformations – physical, emotional, mental and psychological. It is a period in which you are being prepared and equipped with most of what you will need to successfully manage the demands of adult life, one of which is a healthy and stable romantic relationship. For this reason, starting a relationship within this period causes a major upset because you are still in the process of understanding yourself and adapting to the changes taking place in your body and mind.

This challenge of trying to sustain a relationship for which you aren't well-equipped will take a heavy toll on your emotional and psychological health – the result of which will be seen in other areas of your life, especially your studies. Many teenagers find it difficult to concentrate on their studies the moment they get into a romantic relationship. This is because not only do they discover it to be a rollercoaster, up-and-down experience but they also find themselves spending the bulk of their time thinking of the other person or the times shared with them. This is aside from the fact that being in a relationship means having fights over tiny things which also leads to distraction.

Another reason it is not advisable for you to start dating now is that you are at a phase in which you are prone to making mistakes that can affect you for the whole of your lifetime. It may interest you to know that it has been scientifically proven that a critical part of the brain – the prefrontal cortex – is still largely immature in many teenagers. This is the part of the brain that helps with making sound decisions and rational judgments and, curiously, it doesn't become fully developed until about the mid-20s. This means that the teenage years are those in which you are most prone to making mistakes and taking wrong decisions.

Consequently, you shouldn't consider such an important issue as dating because it could lead you into some other actions that could be very costly for your destiny, if not your life.

For instance, there are several cases of young men and women committing suicide because they couldn't handle the pain and shame of being jilted or cheated on. There have also been reports of teenagers committing crimes or going into drugs and other vices just to please the person they claim they are in love with. And in extreme cases, such as the one in the news recently, some teenagers go to the extent of taking their own lives to please their partners.

Last but most importantly is that, since they're still trying to figure out life and their own feelings, what most teenagers define as love at this stage is actually lust for sex and curiosity to explore each other's bodies. Usually when this lust or curiosity is satisfied, disillusionment and boredom set in. This can often lead to broken promises, heartbreaks, depression and even worse!

23

WHY DON'T MY PARENTS ALLOW ME TO GO FOR SLEEPOVERS?

You have to understand that your parents were once teenagers themselves and they are familiar with the mischiefs and problems that teenagers often get into when they go for such sleepovers. Besides, they also often get reports from fellow parents and other sources about the various risks involved in granting teens such permissions. Here, for example, is the regrettable experience of a parent as shared on an online forum:

My youngest daughter (who is now in her early twenties) told me just last week that she now thinks that teenagers should not be allowed to go to sleepovers. She said that she experimented with sex, drugs, and alcohol many times when she was staying at a friend's house. She said she tried pot, lost her virginity, and got drunk for the first time at her friend's house. As you can imagine, I was very surprised about her admitting to those things.

When she was a teenager I can't tell you how many times that I would fight with her and her mother about letting her stay at a friend's house. Her mother thought she should be allowed to but I did not because I could remember all the crap that I got into when I was a kid and saying at a friend's house. So, sometimes she was allowed to go, and sometimes she was not. If I were able to redo raising my teenagers, I can guarantee you they would not be allowed to go stay the night at a friend's house, except under very limited situations and for certain purposes. I would allow them to have friends spend the night at our house where I could keep an eye on them…

With such reports as this and many more, you can easily guess why your parents should be worried. They do not want to spend the rest of their lives regretting that they did not do enough to protect you from youthful lusts and other snares of the youthful age. And of course, they may not be certain that the parents of your friend whose house you want to stay will be as strict about discipline and concerned about safety as they are.

You must understand, though, that denying you sleepovers is not necessarily about your parents not trusting you. It could also be because they are worried about what you might be influenced to do when you are with your friend that you want to stay with or because they are not sure you will be completely safe. As a specialist in criminology once asked, who is to know whether the parent or the boyfriend or girlfriend of the parent or step-parent or someone else living in the house is a drug addict? Who is to know whether the parent or the boyfriend or girlfriend of the parent or step-parent or someone else living in the house is an alcoholic? Who is to know whether the parent or the boyfriend or girlfriend of the parent or step-parent or someone else living in the house allows criminals in the house? Who is to know whether the parent or the boyfriend or girlfriend of the parent or step-parent or someone else living in the house is a fire starter? Or a rapist? Or a serial killer?

You should seriously consider this too, because even if your friend were to be decent and responsible in every way, how can you tell if he or she has a member of the family who can pose a risk to you? Here is how a lady shared her experience: "I was allowed to go over to a sleepover when I was 13 to my best friend's house. During the night sometime the father came stumbling drunk into my friend's bedroom, flipped on the light, looked at me and drunkenly yelled "Who the hell are you?" It scared me to death. I couldn't sleep for the rest of the night..."

It is exactly such scenarios that your parents seek to avoid. In fact, they may have had similar or worse experiences in the past. So, you should try to reason with them and not see them as being overly harsh or protective. They have seen enough to know that they cannot entrust your safety to just anybody else.

So, rather than being angry or bitter over your parents' decision not to let you have sleepovers, do your best to appreciate their efforts, understand their concerns, allay their fears and give them convincing reasons to be sure that they will not regret granting your wish to sleep over. Even if they refused to be convinced, do try to understand that it is all about their love and concern for you, even if you think they are overdoing it. What matters most is that they love you too much to want anything harmful to happen to you. Let this cheer you up!

24

WHY WON'T MY PARENTS LET ME DRIVE THEIR CAR?

There are a number of considerations which could make your parents not want you to drive their car or even drive at all. The first is possession of a valid driver's license. Driving a car isn't just about fun. There are strict legal and safety issues involved. Even if you have mastered some driving skills, your parents won't encourage you to drive without having obtained your driver's license from the relevant government agency.

Since there are critical requirements to be met and tests to be passed before you can be considered qualified and issued a driver's license, driving without one means that you are not qualified to drive and consequently pose a danger to other road users. For this reason, driving without a license is illegal and accordingly attracts severe penalties. These could involve paying a heavy fine, doing community service or even spending some days in jail.

Things can get much worse if you are involved in an accident while doing such illegal driving. If you are involved in a collision or a hit-and-run, for instance, the consequences will be more severe, with additional charges being laid. In addition to the fine you will pay, there is the cost of a lawyer, towing and getting the vehicle out of impound to be considered. That aside, when you eventually get a license, your insurance premium will be significantly affected. As an expert explained, your insurance rates may be affected permanently because when you get your license and purchase insurance on a vehicle, the incident that occurred previously will definitely affect the premium paid. This could result in higher insurance premiums. So, if your parents are not that enthusiastic about you driving, this could be a reason.

Another issue your parents may be concerned about is the financial implication of your driving. To begin with, you cannot drive without having some insurance cover. You must be properly insured if you drive on public road, no matter how short the distance. Even if your parents have given their permission for you to drive the car, and even if they have their own insurance policy covering the vehicle, you still need, at least, third party car insurance if you want to drive. Driving without having this is illegal.

Now, this is where the financial challenge comes in. You have a few options when it comes to insurance policies. First, you can ask your parents to add you as a named driver on their existing policy. This seems like the cheaper and more convenient option in the short-term. Yet, even at that, car-insurance companies automatically raise premiums when a teenager is added to a family's list of drivers. So, your parents are still going to bear some extra financial burden. But this burden gets even heavier if you are to have your own policy.

The third and most important issue your parents are probably concerned about is whether they can trust you enough not to endanger yourself and other road-users and whether you will not get into trouble with traffic rules or misuse their car. Speaking of safety, which is your parents' biggest headache, it has indeed been confirmed that the teenage years are the riskiest when it comes to driving. According to Nichole Morris, a principal researcher at the University of Minnesota, "If you're going to have an early, untimely death, the most dangerous two years of your life are between 16 and 17, and the reason for that is driving."

Morris explained further that among teenagers, death in motor vehicle accidents surpasses suicide, cancer and other types of accidents. "Cars have gotten safer, roads have gotten safer, but teen drivers have not," she said.

You cannot blame Morris for this gloomy outlook on teenage driving. The American Automobile Association (AAA) has the facts and figures to corroborate her submissions. According to a report released by the AAA Foundation for Traffic Safety, "Teen crash rates are higher than any other age group, and this data confirm that the impact of their crashes extend well beyond the teen who is behind the wheel."

The report further said, "In 2013 alone, 371,645 people were injured and 2,927 were killed in crashes that involved a teen driver." So, you can understand why your parents should be concerned about safety.

But then, you may wonder, how does this specifically affect me? Well, that is where the issue of trust comes in. Your parents know you and have spent a much longer time observing you more than anyone else. So they know your character and peculiar tendencies. If you are prone to breaking rules, throwing tantrums or being careless in the way you use things, then they will certainly be worried that this will affect the way you use their car and your attitude to traffic rules and other road-users.

It is therefore important that you put these issues into consideration, and see those you can sort out yourself – especially letting your parents know that they can trust you to be a safe, thoughtful, careful, considerate and law-abiding driver.

25

WHY CAN'T I WATCH ANY MOVIE, LISTEN TO ANY SONG OR READ ANY BOOK I CONSIDER INTERESTING?

That's simply because what you watch, read or listen to gets stored up in your subconscious mind and has a way of influencing your thinking, mood, attitude and behavior over time. Your eyes and ears are the gateways to your mind and it is what you allow into your mind that shapes your mindset, personality and lifestyle, and eventually determines how you end up. This is why it is important that you constantly exercise caution in the choice of books, music, movies and television shows you expose yourself to. As it is said in the world of computers, "garbage in, garbage out."

This caution becomes even more necessary as you realize that there is an agenda being pushed in every song you listen to, every book you read and every movie or show you watch. Yes, behind the obvious fun and entertainment value of these materials are certain powerful messages and influences that are being impressed on people's minds through these channels. Sadly, most of these influences are negative.

Indeed, it has been proven that there is a clear correlation between the violence, immorality, occultism and anti-social behavior portrayed in films, on television, in computer games, in rap lyrics, and other media channels and the violence and antisocial behavior, such as drug use and teenage gun/knife crime, found in real life. Children and teenagers, in particular, are vulnerable to media content because they are still in the early stages of socialization and therefore very impressionable. And in fact, teenagers appear to be the most targeted by most of the producers of media contents!

Over the years, the power of the media in deciding, influencing and shaping people's perceptions and behaviors has been well-known and well-documented. There are even many theories to this effect. One of such is the hypodermic needle (or magic bullet) theory, which says that the media have a direct, immediate and powerful effect on their audiences. The theory suggests that the media could influence a very large group of people directly and uniformly by "shooting" or "injecting" them with appropriate messages designed to trigger a desired response.

It is in knowing this power of communication media that many individuals and groups use music, books and movies to pass across their dangerous messages. Music is particularly employed because it plays an important role in the socialization of children and teenagers. Sadly, the lyrics of most songs have become more explicit in their references to drugs, sex, violence and other criminal behaviors over the years. Same goes for music-videos that have become increasingly characterized by violence, sexually provocative dance moves, sexual stereotypes, and use of substances of abuse. There is hardly any music-video that is produced these days without these immoral contents being glorified.

Many of the movies and television shows being produced in recent times – including cartoons targeted at children – are heavily influenced by people who want to promote Satanism, homosexuality, immoral behaviors and other ungodly lifestyles. There are movies and shows that are brazenly aimed at idolizing Satan and demonism. For instance, in recent years, vampire movies have become blockbusters. Yet, even the literal definition of a "vampire" is a blood-sucking demon.

You may wonder why such a vice as blood-sucking should become popularized in movies. The reason, most times, is to get more and more people possessed with the spirit of darkness, whether willingly – through the deception that it is trendy – or unwillingly, through demonic takeover of their lives.

Some years ago, a young lady confessed to a counselor that she had become addicted to masturbation. According to her, she began the habit after watching a particular movie. She added that she often felt bad each time she masturbated but didn't have the power to prevent it from happening.

You see, that's exactly the goal of most of these producers – to infiltrate your mind with beliefs and behaviors that may prove dangerous to you in the long run. In these days too, many books are designed to promote ungodly beliefs, including occultism. It is for these reasons that you must ensure that whatever books, movies or music that occupy your time and attention are such that are positively enlightening, inspiring, uplifting and edifying.